JOSEPH MIDTHUN   SAMUEL HITI

BUILDING BLOCKS OF SCIENCE

ENERGY

WORLD
BOOK

a Scott Fetzer company
Chicago
www.worldbookonline.com

World Book, Inc.
233 N. Michigan Avenue
Chicago, IL 60601
U.S.A.

For information about other World Book publications, visit our website at http://www.worldbookonline.com or call 1-800-WORLDBK (967-5325).

For information about sales to schools and libraries, call 1-800-975-3250 (United States); 1-800-837-5365 (Canada).

Library of Congress Cataloging-in-Publication Data

Energy.
    p. cm. -- (Building blocks of science)
    Includes index.
    Summary: "A graphic nonfiction volume that introduces energy, including its forms and uses. Features include several photographic pages, a glossary, additional resource list, and an index" --Provided by publisher.
    ISBN 978-0-7166-1422-7
    1. Force and energy--Juvenile literature. I. World Book, Inc.
    QC73.4.E64 2011
    531'.6--dc23
                                    2011025908

Building Blocks of Science
Set ISBN: 978-0-7166-1420-3

Printed in China by Leo Paper Products LTD., Heshan, Guangdong
1st printing December 2011

Acknowledgments:
Created by Samuel Hiti and Joseph Midthun.
Art by Samuel Hiti. Written by Joseph Midthun.

© Dreamstime 10, 11; © Shutterstock 11, 12, 13, 16, 17, 22, 23

ATTENTION, READER!

Some characters in this series throw large objects from tall buildings, play with fire, ride on bicycle handlebars, and perform other dangerous acts. However, they are CARTOON CHARACTERS. Please do not try any of these things at home because you could seriously harm yourself—or others around you!

STAFF

Executive Committee
President: Donald D. Keller
Vice President and Editor in Chief: Paul A. Kobasa
Vice President, Marketing/
    Digital Products: Sean Klunder
Vice President, International: Richard Flower
Director, Human Resources: Bev Ecker

Editorial
Associate Manager, Supplementary
    Publications: Cassie Mayer
Writer and Letterer: Joseph Midthun
Editors: Mike DuRoss and Brian Johnson
Researcher: Annie Brodsky
Manager, Contracts & Compliance
    (Rights & Permissions): Loranne K. Shields

Manufacturing/Pre-Press/Graphics and Design
Director: Carma Fazio
Manufacturing Manager: Steven Hueppchen
Production/Technology Manager:
    Anne Fritzinger
Proofreader: Emilie Schrage
Manager, Graphics and Design: Tom Evans
Coordinator, Design Development and
    Production: Brenda B. Tropinski
Book Design: Samuel Hiti
Photographs Editor: Kathy Creech

TABLE OF CONTENTS

There is a glossary on page 30. Terms defined in the glossary are in type **that looks like this** on their first appearance.

How do you move?

Do you walk, run, or jump?

Do you leap over mountains, fly through the sky, or barrel through brick walls?

If you do, you use me!

I'm ENERGY!

Energy makes things move and do work.

Cars, trains, and airplanes use energy to take us from place to place.

People and animals use energy to live and grow.

Energy is all around us.

The light and heat that you feel from sunshine...

The sounds that you hear around you...

And the electricity that powers lights are all forms of energy!

5

WHAT CAN ENERGY DO?

Energy can set objects in **motion**.

When you push something, you can make it move forward.

When you pull back, you cause it to stop.

Pushing and pulling is the use of energy to move this wheelbarrow.

That's a lot of work!

Energy can also cause an object to change form.

You need to use me if you want to bend **metal**.

TWIST

When you burn wood, the heat energy from the fire turns the wood to ash.

If you apply fire to a pot of water, it will eventually boil.

Heat energy causes the boiling water to change from a liquid into a gas.

whistle

Look at all that energy!

7

WHERE DOES ENERGY COME FROM?

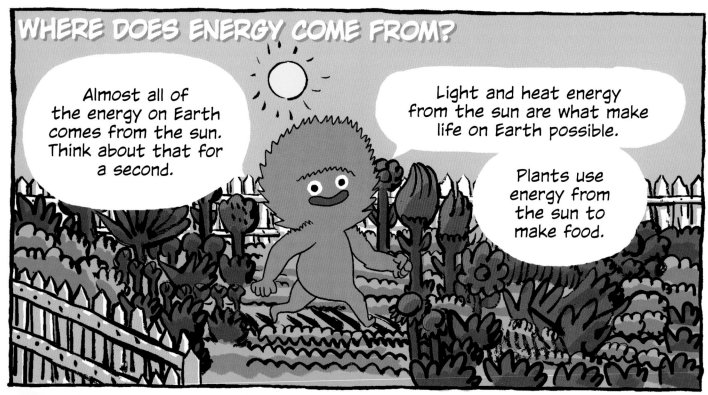

Almost all of the energy on Earth comes from the sun. Think about that for a second.

Light and heat energy from the sun are what make life on Earth possible.

Plants use energy from the sun to make food.

They use this food energy to live and grow.

Many animals eat plants for energy.

You're an animal!

Even animals that eat other animals get their energy from plants.

Without plants to collect this energy, animals would be in serious trouble!

All of the energy in plants comes from the sun.

But what happens to this energy when plants and animals die?

Where does it go?

Worms and other small living things break down the plant and animal **matter**.

This matter releases **nutrients** into the soil that help new plants to grow.

And the cycle of energy continues!

9

FORMS OF ENERGY

Energy comes in many different forms.

Heat energy can heat our homes, run machines, melt materials, and make electricity. We can make heat energy by building fires and mixing chemicals.

You can feel heat energy on a nice day. That heat is coming from the sun!

HEAT ENERGY

Light energy also comes from the sun and objects like lamps or computer screens.

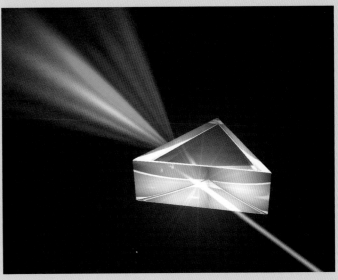

Sound is a form of energy, too. If you read this sentence out loud, you are using sound energy!

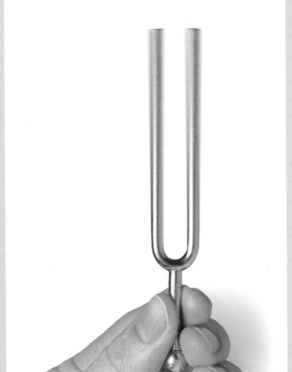

SOUND ENERGY

Motion is another form of energy. Just by turning the page, you're using **kinetic energy.**

You may know electric energy as electricity. Electric energy powers nearly all appliances and electronics in your home.

Have you ever seen electricity in nature? That's right! Lightning is a form of electric energy!

ELECTRIC ENERGY

Chemical energy is what makes transportation possible. Most vehicles burn fuel to release its chemical energy.

Chemical energy flows through your body. It comes from the food you eat.

STORED ENERGY

You know what energy looks like when it's in use.

When I jump over these hurdles...

I'm using kinetic energy to move fast!

WOOHOO!

But energy can be stored for later too! This is called **potential energy**.

Take this wind-up toy.

As I wind it, the spring inside the toy stores the kinetic energy of each turn.

TWIST TWIST TWIST

When the spring is released, its potential energy turns into kinetic energy.

If the spring is released slowly, the dog walks.

YIP   YIP YIP

But if I wind it too tight...

BOING

Humans use potential energy all the time.

This cell phone is powered by a battery.

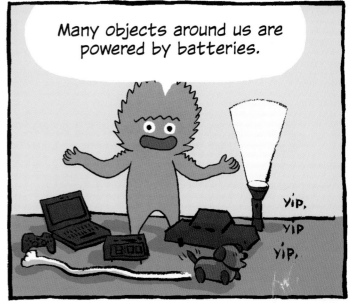

Many objects around us are powered by batteries.

yip.

yip

yip.

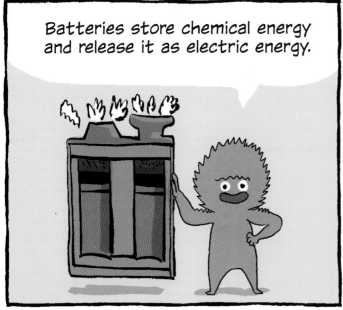

Batteries store chemical energy and release it as electric energy.

Potential energy can also be found in nature.

This piece of coal stores chemical energy.

Scoop

Scoop

When we burn the coal, its chemical energy turns into heat energy.

Potential energy allows us to store energy to use later.

15

CHANGING ENERGY

Another thing you need to know about energy: it's indestructible!

Energy can't be created or destroyed. It simply moves around and changes form.

Can you think of how your body changes energy? How about when you eat?

Your body changes the chemical energy in food into the kinetic energy that you use whenever you move!

You can see changing energy in nature.

This deep-sea jellyfish changes chemical energy into light energy so that it can glow in the dark!

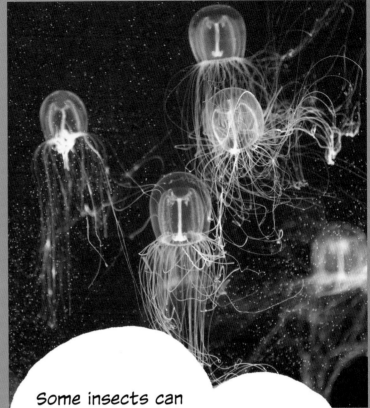

Some insects can change chemical energy into light energy, too. Just look at this firefly...

He is flashing his light to attract mates!

Energy use can be different for every creature!

HOW PEOPLE USE ENERGY

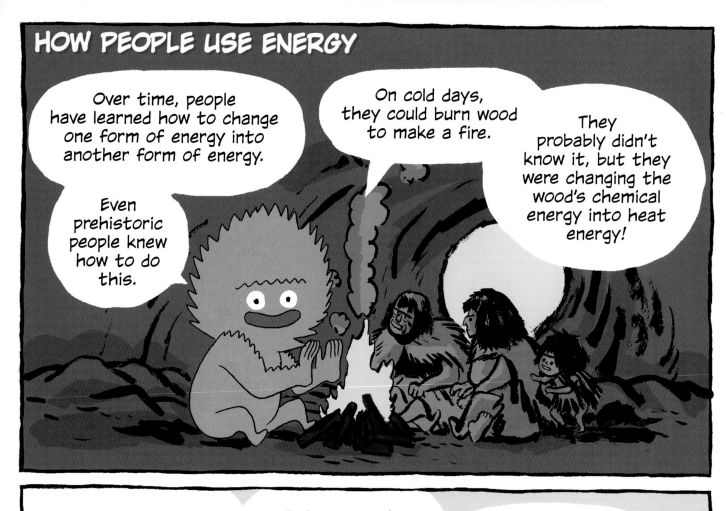

Over time, people have learned how to change one form of energy into another form of energy.

Even prehistoric people knew how to do this.

On cold days, they could burn wood to make a fire.

They probably didn't know it, but they were changing the wood's chemical energy into heat energy!

The ability to change energy into more useful forms is what makes modern life possible.

Today, one of the most useful forms of energy is electric energy.

Look around you. How many things are using electricity?

If there's a computer or TV nearby, you can be sure that they're running on electricity.

And how about your lights?

What about your music player? It uses the stored electricity inside batteries.

Many of the things we do require electricity.

MUSIC

We create this electricity by changing other forms of energy into electric energy.

But it takes an energy source to do so...

FOSSIL FUELS

An energy source is something we can use to make a more useful form of energy.

People use energy sources to make fuel, heat buildings, and to create electricity.

Most of the energy we use comes from burning **fossil fuels**.

Fossil fuels were formed from the remains of living things that died millions of years ago.

Coal, oil, and natural gas are fossil fuels, and they all pack a lot of energy!

Coal is a black or brown rock that can be burned.

Most coal is burned to make electricity.

Natural gas is often burned to heat buildings and cook food.

Oil is made into gasoline for vehicles and fuel oil for homes.

It takes millions of years for fossil fuels to form.

CLUNKA CLUNKA

CLUNKA CLUNKA CLUNKA

Once fossil fuels are used up, they can't be replaced.

That's why people call them **nonrenewable resources.**

21

RENEWABLE RESOURCES

Some energy sources can be used and replaced. They're called **renewable resources.**

Energy from the sun is renewable.

The sun shows up every day!

The sun's energy can be used for heat and to make electric energy.

The sun heats Earth, causing air to move around.

You know this moving air as wind! Wind is a renewable energy source.

Humans use **turbines** to change the energy from wind into electric energy.

Moving water can also be used to make electricity.

Heat from deep inside Earth is also renewable.

Earth has a fiery core that is always hot.

People can use this heat energy to make electric energy or for heating.

GEYSER

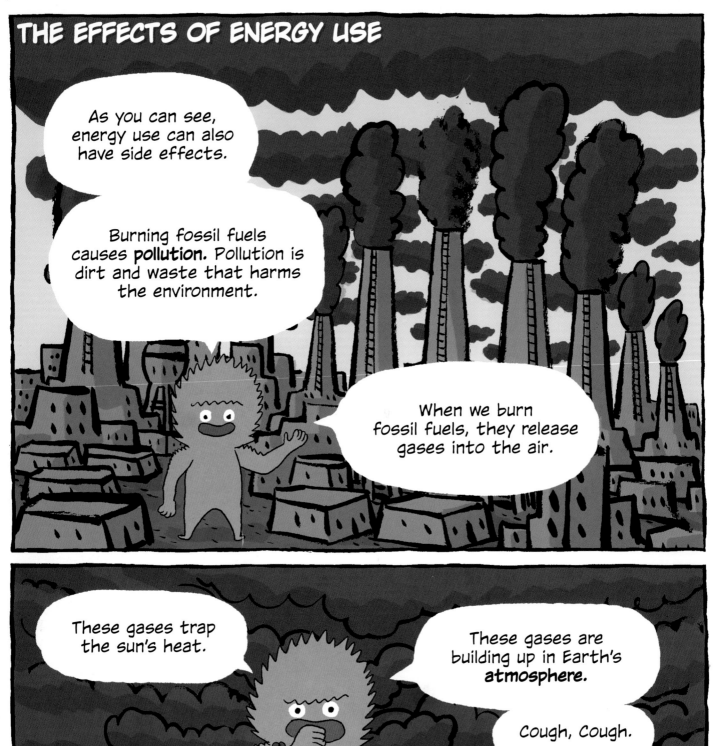

Most scientists believe that Earth is becoming warmer because of these gases.

Acid rain is also caused by pollution in the air. It harms forests, rivers, lakes, and streams, along with the wildlife that lives there.

Smog is a form of air pollution that affects many large cities. Some breathing problems and other human illnesses are caused by smog.

REDUCING ENERGY USE

So what can you do to help reduce our impact on Earth?

You can be energy efficient— like me!

Being energy efficient means using energy wisely.

It also means taking steps to reduce your energy use.

How about turning off the lights when you leave the room?

click

Or reusing and recycling items instead of throwing them away?

glass

Plastic

THE FUTURE OF ENERGY USE

Today, people are working to make renewable energy sources that are as useful as fossil fuels but less harmful.

Every year, scientists create more powerful **solar** panels that collect energy from the sun.

This energy provides a renewable source of electricity.

People have even built airplanes that use solar power!

VRROOM VROOM

Biofuels are fuels made from plants and other natural matter. They can be burned in place of fossil fuels.

Biofuels made from corn are already used in many vehicles.

Scientists are working on fuels made from plants that can grow more easily and quickly than corn.

GLOSSARY

acid rain rain that has become acidic. It is caused by pollution in the air.

atmosphere the mixture of gases in contact with Earth's surface and extending far above.

biofuel any energy-producing substance made from living things.

chemical energy energy that is stored inside the molecules (smallest pieces) of a chemical.

fossil fuel a fuel formed from the long-dead remains of living things. Fossil fuels include coal, natural gas, and petroleum (oil).

kinetic energy the energy of motion.

matter what all things are made of.

metal any of a large group of elements that includes copper, gold, iron, lead, silver, tin, and other elements that share similar qualities.

motion a change in position.

nonrenewable resource a resource that cannot be replenished once it is used up. Fossil fuels are nonrenewable resources.

nutrient a nourishing substance, especially as an element or ingredient of food.

pollution waste and harmful substances produced by human activity and released into the environment.

potential energy energy stored in an object or system that can be converted into kinetic energy.

renewable resource natural resources, such as trees, that can be replaced after they have been used.

smog a form of air pollution that resembles a combination of smoke and fog in the air.

solar of the sun.

turbine an engine or motor in which a wheel is made to revolve by the force of water, steam, hot gases, or air. Turbines are often used to turn generators that produce electric power.

FIND OUT MORE

Books

Energy by Tim Clifford (Rourke Publishing, 2011)

Energy by Kay Manolis (Bellwether Media, 2008)

Energy by Chris Woodford (DK Publishing, 2007)

Energy Everywhere by Patricia Whitehouse (Rourke Publishing, 2007)

Energy and Heat by Kathryn Whyman (Stargazer Books, 2005)

Energy in Motion by Melissa Stewart (Children's Press, 2006)

Energy Makes Things Happen by Kimberly Brubaker Bradley and Paul Meisel (HarperCollins, 2003)

Forms of Energy by Herbert West (PowerKids Press, 2009)

The Shocking Truth About Energy by Loreen Leedy (Holiday House, 2010)

What Is Energy? Exploring Science With Hands-On Activities by Richard Spilsbury and Louise Spilsbury (Enslow Elementary, 2008)

Websites

EcoKids: Get Energy-Wise
http://www.ecokids.ca/pub/eco_info/topics/energy/intro/index.cfm
Learn about what energy is, and how our use of energy affects the planet, at this educational website.

Energy: Fuelling the Future
http://www.sciencemuseum.org.uk/on-line/energy/
Quizzes, games, and stories at this educational website cover sources of energy, how energy works in our lives, and how to conserve energy.

Energy Hogs: Hogbusters Training Camp
http://www.energyhog.org/childrens.htm
At the Hogbusters Training Camp, games and a scavenger hunt will show you different ways of saving energy around your home.

Energy Kids
http://www.eia.gov/kids/
Fun facts about energy can be found at this educational site from the U.S. Energy Information Administration.

Energy Quest
http://energyquest.ca.gov/index.html
At Energy Quest, movies, games, stories, and fact sheets teach the basics of energy—where it comes from, how it works, and how we use it.

Roofus's Solar and Efficient Home
http://www1.eere.energy.gov/kids/roofus/
Learn about the different ways to make your home energy efficient at this website from the U.S. Department of Energy.

Science Kids: Energy Facts
http://www.sciencekids.co.nz/sciencefacts/energy.html
This website offers lists of facts about all different types of energy. Follow the links to learn more about electricity, wind energy, geothermal energy, and even Einstein!

INDEX